How To Play Mandolin

A Comprehensive Guide To Playing The Mandolin With Simple Songs Suitable For Beginners

Copyright@2023

Reginald Canelo

Table Of Content

Introduction 4

    Brief History And Introduction To The Mandolin 4

    The Appeal Of The Mandolin As A Versatile And Beautiful Instrument. 8

    Setting Goals And Expectations For Learning To Play The Mandolin. 12

Chapter 1: Getting Started 16

    Choosing The Right Mandolin: Types, Sizes, And Features. 16

    Understanding The Mandolin's Anatomy. 21

    Properly Holding And Positioning The Mandolin 25

    Tuning The Mandolin 29

Chapter 2: Basic Techniques 32

    Introduction To Picking And Strumming Techniques 32

    Learning To Use A Pick (Plectrum) Effectively 36

Basic Fingerpicking Exercises 41

Understanding Fretting And Finger Placement 44

Chapter 3: Essential Chords and Chord Progressions 48

Learning Common Chords Used In Mandolin Playing 48

Practicing Chord Transitions And Progressions 52

Chapter 4: Melodies And Single Note Playing 55

Learning To Play Simple Melodies On The Mandolin 55

Chapter 5: Rhythm And Strumming Patterns 64

Understanding Different Rhythm Patterns 64

Developing A Sense Of Timing And Groove 68

Strumming Techniques For Different Music Styles 72

Chapter 6: Advanced Techniques 77

Introduction To Advanced Techniques Like Tremolo, Slides, And Hammer-Ons. 77

Developing Speed And Accuracy In Playing..................................81

Chapter 7: Playing Simple Melody Songs On The Mandolin..85

1. "Twinkle, Twinkle, Little Star" - A classic nursery rhyme melody..............85

2. "You Are My Sunshine" - A simple and heartwarming folk song.................90

3. "Amazing Grace" - A beautiful and well-known hymn................................94

5. "Scarborough Fair" - A traditional English ballad with an easy chord progression. 101

6. "Wildwood Flower" - A classic bluegrass tune with simple picking patterns. 105

7. "House of the Rising Sun" - A haunting folk song made famous by The Animals. 109

Chapter 8: Maintenance And Care 113

Cleaning, Restringing, And Adjusting The Instrument 117

Dealing With Common Issues And Troubleshooting 123

Introduction

Brief History And Introduction To The Mandolin

The mandolin is a beautiful and versatile stringed instrument with a rich history dating back several centuries. Here's a brief overview of the history and introduction to the mandolin:

History:

The roots of the mandolin can be traced back to ancient civilizations, with early variations of the instrument appearing in different forms across various cultures. The modern mandolin, as we know it today, evolved in Italy during the 17th and 18th centuries. Its direct ancestor is the mandola, a larger instrument from the lute family.

The mandolin's popularity grew during the 19th century, particularly in Naples, Italy, where it became an essential part of the Neapolitan folk music tradition. Its compact size and bright, expressive sound made it well-suited for both solo performances and ensemble playing.

In the late 19th and early 20th centuries, Italian immigrants brought the mandolin to the United States, where it gained popularity in various musical styles, including folk, country, and bluegrass. It became a key instrument in the development of American roots music.

Introduction:

The mandolin is a member of the lute family and features a pear-shaped body with a flat top, a short neck with frets, and four pairs of metal strings. The strings are typically tuned in unison, meaning each pair of strings is tuned to the same pitch.

Modern mandolins come in various styles and sizes, with the most common being the bowl-back and the flat-back. The bowl-back mandolin has a rounded, bowl-shaped back, while the flat-back mandolin has a flat back similar to that of a guitar. The mandolin's sound is bright, sweet, and resonant, making it suitable for a wide range of musical genres.

Playing the mandolin involves both picking and strumming techniques. Players use a pick (plectrum) to pluck the strings individually or in combination to create melodies, chords, and intricate patterns. It is also common for mandolin players to use their fingers for fingerpicking, which allows for greater expressiveness and control.

The mandolin has found its place in various musical genres, including classical, bluegrass, folk, country, and even rock and pop music. Its versatility has made it a beloved instrument among musicians worldwide, and its unique sound continues to captivate audiences to this day.

Whether you're a beginner or an experienced musician, the mandolin offers a rewarding musical journey with its distinct charm and wide range of playing styles.

The Appeal Of The Mandolin As A Versatile And Beautiful Instrument.

The mandolin's appeal lies in its unique combination of versatility and beauty, making it a captivating and cherished instrument for musicians and audiences alike. Here are some key aspects that contribute to the mandolin's allure:

1. Unique Sound: The mandolin produces a distinct, bright, and sweet sound that sets it apart from other stringed instruments. Its timbre is both vibrant and delicate, creating a captivating and enchanting tone that resonates with listeners.

2. Versatility: Despite its small size, the mandolin is incredibly versatile and can be found in a wide range of musical genres. From classical to folk, bluegrass to rock, the mandolin can adapt and enhance the sound of various styles, making it a valuable addition to any ensemble or musical setting.

3. Expressiveness: The mandolin offers a wide range of expressive techniques, allowing musicians to convey emotions and feelings through their playing. From gentle and melodic to lively and energetic, the mandolin's expressiveness allows for a broad palette of musical expression.

4. Portability: One of the practical advantages of the mandolin is its portability. Its compact size makes it easy to carry around, making it a popular instrument for musicians on the go or for those who want to play music in social gatherings or jam sessions.

5. Charming Aesthetics: The mandolin's elegant design, with its pear-shaped body and intricate craftsmanship, contributes to its aesthetic appeal. It is often regarded as a visually appealing instrument, attracting attention and admiration.

6. Harmonic Accompaniment: In addition to playing melodies, the mandolin is also well-suited for chordal accompaniment, making it an ideal instrument for both solo performances and ensemble playing. Its bright sound cuts through the mix, adding a unique layer to the music.

7. Community and Tradition: The mandolin has a strong association with community and tradition, especially in folk and bluegrass music. It is often seen as a symbol of cultural heritage and brings people together through shared musical experiences.

8. Learning Curve: For aspiring musicians, the mandolin offers a manageable learning curve, especially for those already familiar with other stringed instruments like the guitar. Its fretted fingerboard and standard tuning make it relatively easy to start playing and learning basic songs.

Setting Goals And Expectations For Learning To Play The Mandolin.

Setting clear goals and realistic expectations is crucial when learning to play the mandolin, as it helps keep you motivated and focused on your musical journey. Here are some guidelines for setting goals and expectations:

1. Identify Your Motivation: Start by understanding why you want to learn the mandolin. Are you drawn to a specific genre, looking to play in a band, or simply want a new hobby? Knowing your motivation will guide your learning path.

2. Define Short-term and Long-term Goals: Set achievable short-term goals, such as learning a particular chord progression or playing a simple melody. Simultaneously, establish long-term goals, like performing a specific song or mastering a particular playing technique. Divide your learning process into smaller milestones to track your progress effectively.

3. Be Realistic: Recognize that learning to play the mandolin takes time and practice. Avoid expecting immediate perfection and understand that improvement comes gradually. Be patient with yourself, and celebrate each small achievement along the way.

4. Practice Regularly: Consistency is key to progress. Create a practice schedule that suits your lifestyle and commit to it. Even dedicating a few minutes each day can make a significant difference over time.

5. Focus on Fundamentals: Prioritize building a strong foundation. Learn essential techniques, scales, chords, and music theory. These fundamentals will form the backbone of your mandolin skills and enable you to tackle more advanced concepts later on.

6. Diversify Your Repertoire: Explore different musical styles and genres. Learning a variety of songs will keep your practice sessions engaging and help you become a well-rounded mandolin player.

7. Enjoy the Process: Learning to play the mandolin should be enjoyable and fulfilling. Don't get discouraged by challenges or mistakes. Embrace the learning process and find joy in the progress you make, no matter how small.

8. Join a Community: Engage with other mandolin players, either in-person or online. Participating in music groups, workshops, or forums can provide support, inspiration, and opportunities to collaborate.

9. Set Performance Goals: Performing in front of others, even in informal settings, can boost your confidence and help you refine your skills. Consider setting performance goals, such as playing for friends or family or participating in open-mic events.

Chapter 1: Getting Started

Choosing The Right Mandolin: Types, Sizes, And Features.

Choosing the right mandolin involves considering various factors such as the type of mandolin, its size, and the specific features that suit your musical preferences and playing style. Here's a guide to help you make an informed decision:

Types of Mandolins:
1. A-Style Mandolin: A-Style mandolins have a teardrop-shaped body with a round soundhole. They are generally considered more aesthetically pleasing and are popular among folk and classical players.

2. F-Style Mandolin: F-Style mandolins have a more ornate design with an extended scroll on the body and an f-shaped soundhole. They often have a richer tone and are commonly used in bluegrass and country music.

3. Bowl-Back Mandolin: Also known as round-back mandolins, these instruments have a rounded, bowl-shaped back. They are more common in European and Mediterranean folk music.

Sizes of Mandolins:
1. Standard Size: This is the most common size, suitable for most players, and is what you'll find in most mandolin models.

2. Octave Mandolin (Mandola): Larger than the standard mandolin, it produces a lower pitch and is often used for accompaniment in ensembles.

3. Mandocello: Even larger than the octave mandolin, the mandocello produces an even lower pitch, similar to a cello.

Features to Consider:
1. Tone Woods: The type of wood used in the construction of the mandolin significantly influences its tone. Common woods include spruce, cedar, maple, and mahogany. Each wood imparts its unique characteristics to the instrument's sound.

2. Fretboard and Frets: Consider the width and length of the fretboard. A wider fretboard might be more comfortable for fingerpicking, while a narrower one may be preferable for faster playing.

3. Number of Frets: Standard mandolins typically have 20 frets. Some models offer extended fretboards with 22 or more frets, providing a broader tonal range.

4. Bridge and Tailpiece: These components affect the mandolin's sustain and intonation. Adjustable bridges and tailpieces allow for fine-tuning and optimization of the instrument's playability.

5. Pickup System (if required): If you plan to play the mandolin amplified, consider models with built-in pickups or the option to install one.

6. Brand and Reputation: Research different mandolin brands and read reviews to assess their reputation for producing quality instruments.

7. Playability: Before making a purchase, try out the mandolin to ensure it feels comfortable in your hands and suits your playing style.

8. Budget: Set a budget range and explore mandolins within that range. While higher-quality instruments may come with a higher price tag, there are also decent beginner-level mandolins available at more affordable prices.

Understanding The Mandolin's Anatomy.

Understanding the anatomy of the mandolin is essential for learning to play and maintain the instrument effectively. Here are the key components of a typical mandolin:

1. Headstock: The headstock is located at the top end of the mandolin's neck. It houses the tuning pegs or machine heads, which are used to adjust the tension of the strings and tune the instrument.

2. Nut: The nut is a small piece of material (usually plastic, bone, or ivory) situated at the end of the fingerboard, near the headstock. It has grooves that hold the strings in position and determine their spacing.

3. Tuning Pegs: Also known as machine heads or tuning machines, these are attached to the headstock. Turning the tuning pegs adjusts the tension of the strings to raise or lower their pitch.

4. Neck: The neck is the long, slender portion of the mandolin that extends from the headstock to the body. It typically has a fretted fingerboard on top, which is where the player presses down on the strings to produce different notes.

5. Fretboard: The fretboard is a flat or slightly curved surface on top of the neck. It contains metal frets embedded across the fingerboard, determining the pitch of each note when a string is pressed against them.

6. Frets: Frets are thin metal bars embedded in the fretboard at specific intervals. When the strings are pressed down between two frets, they produce different pitches, allowing the player to play different notes and chords.

7. Soundhole: The soundhole is a round or f-shaped opening in the body of the mandolin, usually located below the strings. It allows the sound to resonate and project from the instrument.

8. Body: The body is the main resonating chamber of the mandolin. It can have different shapes, such as teardrop (A-style) or extended teardrop with scroll (F-style). The body is where the sound is amplified and projected.

9. Bridge: The bridge is a small, flat piece of material (often wood) located on the face of the mandolin, near the soundhole. The strings pass over the bridge, transmitting their vibrations to the soundboard and body.

10. Tailpiece: The tailpiece is located at the bottom end of the mandolin and anchors the strings to the instrument. It keeps the strings secure and provides a fixed point for adjusting string tension.

11. Pickguard: The pickguard is a protective plate made of plastic or other materials that is placed below the strings, near the soundhole. It helps protect the finish of the mandolin from scratches caused by the player's pick.

12. Strings: The mandolin typically has eight strings, arranged in four pairs (known as courses). The pairs are tuned in unison, meaning each pair has two strings of the same pitch.

Properly Holding And Positioning The Mandolin

Properly holding and positioning the mandolin is crucial for both playing comfort and achieving the best sound from the instrument. Here's a step-by-step guide to help you with the correct mandolin holding and positioning:

1. Sitting or Standing: You can play the mandolin while sitting or standing. If sitting, use a sturdy chair without arms to allow free movement of your arms. If standing, use a comfortable shoulder strap to support the mandolin's weight.

2. Positioning the Mandolin: Hold the mandolin on your lap (if sitting) or against your body (if standing). The instrument's back should rest against your abdomen, and the neck should extend towards your left hand (if you're right-handed).

3. Support with Forearm: Place your right forearm (for right-handed players) on the mandolin's body to support it. This provides stability and control while playing.

4. Positioning the Fretting Hand: Curve your left-hand fingers and place them on the fretboard to press down the strings. Your thumb should rest against the back of the neck, providing support and stability. Avoid pressing too hard; a light touch is usually sufficient to produce clean notes.

5. Positioning the Picking Hand: Your right-hand fingers will be used for picking or strumming the strings. Some players prefer using a pick (plectrum), while others use their fingers (fingerpicking). Experiment and find what works best for you. Maintain a relaxed hand position and avoid excessive tension in your picking hand.

6. Elbow Position: Both arms should be relaxed. The right elbow (picking hand) should be comfortably away from your body, allowing your hand to move freely across the strings. The left elbow (fretting hand) should also be relaxed and positioned in a way that allows easy access to all frets.

7. Mandolin Angle: Tilt the mandolin slightly upward so that the soundhole faces you. This angle helps direct the sound towards your ears, making it easier to hear your playing.

8. Relaxed Posture: Maintain a relaxed and comfortable posture while playing. Avoid hunching over or tensing your shoulders.

This will help prevent fatigue during long playing sessions.

9. Practice and Adjust: As you start playing, you may find some adjustments are needed to achieve the most comfortable and natural playing position for yourself. Experiment with different angles and hand positions to find what feels best for you.

Tuning The Mandolin

Tuning a mandolin is essential to ensure that it produces the correct pitches and sounds in harmony with other instruments. The standard tuning for a mandolin is G-D-A-E, with pairs of strings tuned to the same note, as follows:

1. G (lowest pitch) - Pair of strings, both tuned to G
2. D - Pair of strings, both tuned to D
3. A - Pair of strings, both tuned to A
4. E (highest pitch) - Pair of strings, both tuned to E

To tune your mandolin, you can follow these steps:

1. Use a Tuner: The easiest and most accurate way to tune your mandolin is by using an electronic tuner. There are various tuners available that can clip onto the headstock of the mandolin or be used as smartphone apps. Pluck each string one at a time, and adjust the tuning peg until the tuner indicates that the pitch is correct.

2. Tuning by Ear: If you don't have a tuner available, you can tune your mandolin by ear using a reference pitch. One common method is to use a piano or keyboard to provide the reference pitches. Start by tuning the A string to the A above middle C on the piano. Once you have the A string in tune, you can tune the other strings relative to it.

- To tune the D string, play the 7th fret of the A string (the note D) and tune the D string until it matches that pitch.

- To tune the G string, play the 7th fret of the D string (the note G) and tune the G string until it matches that pitch.
- To tune the E string, play the 7th fret of the G string (the note E) and tune the E string until it matches that pitch.

3. Fine-tuning: After you've tuned the mandolin, it's a good idea to go through the strings again, plucking each one and making any necessary fine-tuning adjustments using your ear or a tuner until all the strings are in tune with each other.

Chapter 2: Basic Techniques

Introduction To Picking And Strumming Techniques

Picking and strumming are two fundamental techniques used to produce sound on the mandolin. Whether you want to play melodies, chords, or accompany songs, mastering these techniques is essential for becoming a well-rounded mandolin player. Let's delve into the basics of picking and strumming:

1. Picking Technique:
   - **Downstroke:** To perform a downstroke, use your pick (or fingers) to strike the strings in a downward motion towards the floor. This is denoted by the symbol "↓" in music notation.

- Upstroke: An upstroke is the opposite of a downstroke. Use your pick (or fingers) to strike the strings in an upward motion towards the ceiling. This is denoted by the symbol "↑" in music notation.

- Alternate Picking: Alternate picking involves combining downstrokes and upstrokes in a continuous and even pattern. It is a common technique used to play fast and accurate passages.

- Crosspicking: Crosspicking is a picking technique where the pick moves across multiple strings in a specific pattern, often used in bluegrass and other styles.

2. Strumming Technique:
- **Downward Strum:** For a downward strum, position your pick (or fingers) above the strings and brush them in a downward

motion. This produces a full sound with all the strings being strummed.

- Upward Strum: An upward strum is similar to a downward strum, but the motion is in the opposite direction, strumming upwards across the strings.

- Strumming Patterns: Strumming patterns involve specific combinations of downstrokes and upstrokes, creating rhythmic patterns that fit the song's tempo and style.

3. Using Both Techniques:
- Picking and strumming can be combined to add variety and texture to your playing. For example, you can use picking to play a melody while incorporating strumming for chord accompaniment.

4. Practice Tips:

- Start with slow and simple patterns to develop accuracy and control.

- Focus on maintaining a steady rhythm and staying in time with a metronome or backing track.

- Gradually increase the speed and complexity of your picking and strumming patterns as you progress.

5. Experiment and Explore:

- There are various picking and strumming patterns to discover, depending on the style of music you want to play. Experiment with different techniques and find what works best for you.

Learning To Use A Pick (Plectrum) Effectively

Learning to use a pick (plectrum) effectively is crucial for many mandolin players, as it enables you to achieve a clear and consistent sound. Here are some tips to help you use a pick effectively on the mandolin:

1. Choose the Right Pick:
   - Picks come in various materials, sizes, and thicknesses. Experiment with different picks to find the one that feels comfortable and suits your playing style.
   - Generally, thinner picks are more flexible and produce a lighter sound, while thicker picks offer more control and produce a stronger sound.

2. Hold the Pick Correctly:

- Hold the pick between your thumb and index finger with the pointed end facing downward.

- Keep a relaxed grip on the pick, avoiding excessive tension in your hand and fingers.

3. Control the Angle:

- Angle the pick slightly, so the pointed end is at a slight angle to the strings. This will help you achieve a smoother and more fluid motion while picking.

4. Start Slowly:

- Begin by practicing simple picking exercises or playing individual notes on the mandolin with the pick. Focus on accuracy and precision.

5. Practice Alternate Picking:

- Alternate picking involves using a downstroke followed by an upstroke and is commonly used for playing melodies and fast passages.

- Practice picking individual strings with alternate picking to develop evenness and coordination.

6. Work on Strumming:

- If you're using a pick for strumming, practice strumming patterns at a slow pace and gradually increase the speed as you become more comfortable.

- Ensure that the pick strikes all the strings evenly during strumming to achieve a balanced and pleasing sound.

7. Practice String Crossing:

- Work on smoothly transitioning from one string to another with the pick. This skill is essential for playing melodies and chords across different strings.

8. Use Your Wrist and Arm:

 - When picking, use a combination of wrist and arm movements. Avoid relying solely on finger movements, as this may cause tension and reduce fluidity.

9. Control Dynamics:

 - Vary your picking pressure to control the dynamics (volume) of your playing. Lighten your grip for softer passages and increase pressure for louder sections.

10. Record Yourself:

 - Record yourself while practicing with a pick. Listen to your recordings to identify areas for improvement and monitor your progress over time.

11. Be Patient and Consistent:

- Learning to use a pick effectively takes time and practice. Be patient with yourself and practice regularly to build your pick control and technique.

Basic Fingerpicking Exercises

Fingerpicking exercises are an excellent way to improve your finger dexterity, coordination, and control on the mandolin. These exercises will also help you develop a strong foundation for more complex fingerpicking patterns in the future. Here are some basic fingerpicking exercises to get you started:

Exercise 1: Alternating Thumb Pattern

1. Place your right-hand thumb (if you're right-handed) on the G string (the lowest-pitched string).
2. Place your index finger on the E string (the highest-pitched string).
3. Pluck the G string with your thumb and then pluck the E string with your index finger.

4. Repeat this pattern: thumb (G string), index (E string), thumb (G string), index (E string), and so on.

Exercise 2: Two-Finger Pattern

1. Place your right-hand thumb on the G string and your index finger on the D string (the string above the G string).
2. Pluck the G string with your thumb and then pluck the D string with your index finger.
3. Repeat this pattern: thumb (G string), index (D string), thumb (G string), index (D string), and so on.

Exercise 3: Four-Finger Pattern

1. Place your right-hand thumb on the G string, index finger on the D string, middle finger on the A string (the string above the D string), and ring finger on the E string.

2. Pluck the G string with your thumb, D string with your index finger, A string with your middle finger, and E string with your ring finger.

3. Repeat this pattern: thumb (G string), index (D string), middle (A string), ring (E string), thumb (G string), index (D string), middle (A string), ring (E string), and so on.

Exercise 4: Arpeggio Pattern

1. Choose a simple chord, like a C major or G major chord.

2. Pluck the notes of the chord one at a time in sequence: start with the lowest-pitched string of the chord, then move to the next higher-pitched string, and so on.

3. Repeat this arpeggio pattern: lowest note, next note, next note, and so on.

Understanding Fretting And Finger Placement

Understanding fretting and finger placement on the mandolin is crucial for producing clear and accurate notes. Fretting refers to the act of pressing the strings against the fretboard to change the pitch of the strings and play different notes and chords. Here's a step-by-step guide to fretting and finger placement:

1. Finger Numbering:
   - Index finger: Often referred to as "1"
   - Middle finger: Often referred to as "2"
   - Ring finger: Often referred to as "3"
   - Pinky finger: Often referred to as "4"

2. Positioning Your Hand:

- Place your thumb behind the neck of the mandolin, allowing your fingers to reach the fretboard comfortably.

- Keep your fingers slightly curved, like a gentle claw, to ensure each fingertip presses down on the strings correctly.

3. Finger Placement:

- When fretting a note, press down the string directly against the fret (the metal bar embedded in the fretboard).

- Avoid pressing the string on the fret itself, as this can create unwanted buzzing or muffled sound.

- Position your finger close to the fret, but not on top of it, to achieve clear and accurate notes.

4. Tips for Finger Placement:

- Use the very tips of your fingers to press down the strings. This reduces the chance of accidentally muting adjacent strings.

- Keep your fingers as close to the fret as possible without touching it for optimal intonation and sound clarity.

- Place your fingers down firmly enough to produce a clean note but not so hard that it causes discomfort or unnecessary tension in your hand.

5. Playing Chords:

- When playing chords, try to arch your fingers slightly to avoid touching neighboring strings that should remain open.

- Practice transitioning between chords smoothly, lifting your fingers just enough to move to the next chord without lifting them too far away from the fretboard.

6. Hand and Wrist Position:

- Maintain a relaxed hand and wrist position to prevent strain and fatigue while playing.

- Avoid bending your wrist excessively, keeping it in a neutral and comfortable position.

Chapter 3: Essential Chords and Chord Progressions

Learning Common Chords Used In Mandolin Playing

Learning common chords on the mandolin is a fundamental skill for playing a wide variety of songs and styles. Here are some of the most common chords used in mandolin playing:

1. G Major (G):

   - E string: Open
   - A string: 2nd fret (with the index finger)

2. C Major (C):

   - A string: 3rd fret (with the ring finger)
   - D string: 2nd fret (with the middle finger)
   - G string: Open
   - E string: 1st fret (with the index finger)

3. D Major (D):

- D string: Open
- A string: 2nd fret (with the index finger)
- E string: 2nd fret (with the ring finger)

4. A Major (A):

- A string: Open
- E string: 1st fret (with the index finger)
- G string: 1st fret (with the middle finger)

5. E Major (E):

- E string: Open
- A string: 2nd fret (with the index finger)
- D string: 2nd fret (with the middle finger)
- G string: 1st fret (with the ring finger)

6. F Major (F):

- E string: 1st fret (with the index finger)
- A string: 3rd fret (with the ring finger)
- D string: 3rd fret (with the pinky finger)
- G string: 2nd fret (with the middle finger)

7. D Minor (Dm):

  - D string: Open

  - A string: 1st fret (with the index finger)

  - E string: 2nd fret (with the ring finger)

8. A Minor (Am):

  - A string: Open

  - E string: 1st fret (with the index finger)

  - G string: 2nd fret (with the middle finger)

9. C Major 7 (CM7):

  - A string: 3rd fret (with the ring finger)

  - D string: 2nd fret (with the middle finger)

  - G string: 2nd fret (with the index finger)

  - E string: Open

10. G7:

  - E string: Open

  - A string: 2nd fret (with the index finger)

  - G string: 2nd fret (with the middle finger)

  - D string: 0 (Open)

These chords are just a starting point, and there are many more chords to explore on the mandolin. Practice transitioning between these chords smoothly and accurately to build your chord vocabulary and increase your versatility as a mandolin player. Additionally, learning different chord variations (e.g., adding seventh or minor chords) will allow you to play more complex and interesting chord progressions in your favorite songs.

Practicing Chord Transitions And Progressions

Building on the previous list, here are some additional common chords used in mandolin playing:

1. B Major (B):
   - A string: 2nd fret (with the index finger)
   - D string: 4th fret (with the ring finger)
   - G string: 4th fret (with the pinky finger)

2. E Minor (Em):
   - E string: Open
   - A string: 2nd fret (with the index finger)
   - D string: 2nd fret (with the middle finger)

3. A7:
   - A string: Open
   - D string: 2nd fret (with the index finger)
   - G string: 0 (Open)

- E string: 2nd fret (with the ring finger)

4. D7:

- D string: Open

- A string: 2nd fret (with the index finger)

- G string: 2nd fret (with the middle finger)

- E string: Open

5. E7:

- E string: Open

- A string: 2nd fret (with the index finger)

- D string: 1st fret (with the middle finger)

- G string: 2nd fret (with the ring finger)

6. B7:

- A string: 2nd fret (with the index finger)

- D string: 4th fret (with the ring finger)

- G string: 2nd fret (with the middle finger)

- E string: 2nd fret (with the pinky finger)

7. F# Major (F#):

- D string: 4th fret (with the index finger)
- A string: 4th fret (with the middle finger)
- E string: 2nd fret (with the ring finger)

8. G Minor (Gm):

- G string: Open
- D string: 0 (Open)
- A string: 1st fret (with the index finger)

9. C7:

- A string: 3rd fret (with the ring finger)
- D string: 2nd fret (with the middle finger)
- G string: 3rd fret (with the pinky finger)
- E string: 1st fret (with the index finger)

10. Dm7:

- D string: Open
- A string: 1st fret (with the index finger)
- G string: 2nd fret (with the middle finger)
- E string: 1st fret (with the ring finger)

Chapter 4: Melodies And Single Note Playing

Learning To Play Simple Melodies On The Mandolin

Learning to play simple melodies on the mandolin is an excellent starting point for beginners. It allows you to get familiar with the instrument, develop finger dexterity, and lay the foundation for more advanced playing. Here's a step-by-step guide to help you learn simple melodies on the mandolin:

1. Know the Basics:

   - Familiarize yourself with the parts of the mandolin, the names of the strings, and proper hand positioning.

   - Learn how to hold the pick (plectrum) correctly, if you plan to use one.

2. Start with Easy Melodies:

- Choose simple melodies from familiar tunes, nursery rhymes, or folk songs. Look for songs that have straightforward note patterns and limited range.

3. Use Mandolin Tablature (Tab):

- Mandolin tablature is a visual representation of the mandolin's fretboard, indicating which frets and strings to play for each note.

- Find mandolin tabs for the melodies you want to learn. Many websites and resources offer free mandolin tabs for popular tunes.

4. Practice Each Phrase:

- Break the melody down into smaller phrases or segments. Practice each phrase separately before putting them together.

- Focus on accurate finger placement and rhythm while playing each phrase.

5. Use a Metronome:

   - Use a metronome to maintain a steady tempo and improve your sense of timing. Start at a slower pace and gradually increase the tempo as you become more comfortable.

6. Master Finger Placement:

   - Pay attention to proper finger placement on the fretboard. Use the very tips of your fingers to press down on the strings, and avoid touching adjacent strings unintentionally.

7. Practice Slowly and Gradually Increase Speed:

   - Begin practicing at a slow tempo to ensure accuracy. As you gain confidence, gradually increase the speed while maintaining control.

8. Experiment with Dynamics:

   - Add dynamics (loudness and softness) to your playing to make the melody more expressive. Experiment with playing certain notes louder and others softer.

9. Record Yourself:

   - Record yourself playing the melodies. Listening to the recordings will help you identify areas for improvement and track your progress over time.

10. Be Patient and Persistent:

   - Learning to play melodies takes time and practice. Be patient with yourself and stay consistent with your practice sessions.

11. Explore Different Genres:

   - Practice melodies from various genres, such as classical, folk, bluegrass, or pop.

This will expose you to different musical styles and techniques.

Practicing Scales And Exercises For Finger Dexterity

Practicing scales and exercises for finger dexterity is essential for developing the agility, speed, and precision needed to become a proficient mandolin player. Here are some useful scale exercises to improve finger dexterity:

1. Major Scale Exercise:

- Start with the G major scale, as it is one of the most common scales used on the mandolin.

- Play the G major scale ascending (going up) and descending (going down) in one position.

- Repeat the exercise starting from different positions on the fretboard.

2. Chromatic Scale Exercise:

- Play the chromatic scale using all four fingers on one string, moving up and down the fretboard.

- Repeat the exercise on each string, gradually increasing the speed.

3. Finger Spider Exercise:

- Place your fingers on four consecutive frets (e.g., 1st, 2nd, 3rd, and 4th frets) of one string.

- Play each finger in sequence (1-2-3-4) and then reverse the order (4-3-2-1) while maintaining a steady rhythm.

4. Two-Finger Per String Exercise:

- Choose a scale (e.g., G major) and play it using only two fingers per string.

- Start with your index finger on the lower string and your ring finger on the higher string.

5. Four-Finger Per String Exercise:

   - Practice the G major scale using all four fingers on each string.

   - This exercise challenges your finger coordination and stretches your hand across the fretboard.

6. String Skipping Exercise:

   - Create a sequence that involves skipping strings. For example, play a note on the G string, skip the D string, play a note on the A string, skip the E string, and so on.

7. Alternating Fingers Exercise:

   - Play a repetitive sequence of notes using alternating fingers (e.g., index and middle fingers).

   - This exercise helps develop evenness and balance between your fingers.

8. Trill Exercise:

- Practice trilling between two adjacent notes on a single string using two fingers (e.g., index and middle fingers).

- Start slowly and increase the speed as you gain control.

Chapter 5: Rhythm And Strumming Patterns

Understanding Different Rhythm Patterns

Understanding different rhythm patterns is essential for adding variety and dynamics to your mandolin playing. Rhythm patterns dictate the timing and duration of notes, rests, and accents, giving music its distinctive groove and feel. Here are some common rhythm patterns and their explanations:

1. Basic Downstrokes:
   - Strum all the strings in a downward direction using a single motion. This creates a simple and steady rhythm commonly used in folk and country music.

2. Basic Upstrokes:

- Strum all the strings in an upward direction using a single motion. This is often used to add variety to downstroke-heavy rhythms.

3. Down-Up Strumming:

- Alternate between downstrokes and upstrokes in a continuous pattern. This is a common rhythm used in various music genres.

4. Eighth Note Strumming:

- Divide each beat into two equal parts, and strum on both the downstroke and upstroke for each beat. This creates a faster and more energetic rhythm.

5. Sixteenth Note Strumming:

- Divide each beat into four equal parts, and strum four times per beat, alternating between downstrokes and upstrokes. This creates a very fast and lively rhythm.

6. Syncopation:

- Emphasize off-beats or weak beats to create a sense of rhythmic tension and excitement. This is commonly used in jazz, blues, and funk music.

7. Swing Rhythm:

- Commonly used in jazz and some folk styles, swing rhythm involves altering the timing of eighth notes to create a "swung" or syncopated feel.

8. Triplets:

- Divide each beat into three equal parts, and play three notes in the space of one beat. This creates a unique and syncopated rhythm.

9. Arpeggios:

- Play the notes of a chord one after another instead of strumming them simultaneously. This creates a flowing and melodic rhythm.

10. Dotted Rhythms:

- Extend the duration of a note by half its original value, creating a "dot" after the note. This adds a sense of rhythmic interest and accents to the music.

11. Staccato:

- Play the notes in a short and detached manner, with minimal sustain. This creates a sharp and crisp rhythm.

12. Legato:

- Play the notes smoothly and connected to create a flowing and sustained rhythm.

Developing A Sense Of Timing And Groove

Developing a sense of timing and groove is essential for any musician, including mandolin players. A strong sense of timing and groove will make your playing more enjoyable and help you play with other musicians more effectively. Here are some tips to develop your sense of timing and groove on the mandolin:

1. Practice with a Metronome:

  - Use a metronome to practice playing along with a steady beat. Start with a slow tempo and gradually increase the speed as you become more comfortable.

  - Focus on playing precisely in time with the metronome, ensuring that your notes align with the beats.

2. Tap Your Foot or Use Body Movement:

- Tap your foot or sway with the music as you play. This physical movement can help internalize the rhythm and keep you in sync with the groove.

3. Listen to Different Styles of Music:

- Listen to a variety of music genres and pay attention to the rhythm and groove of each. Try to identify the rhythmic patterns and how they contribute to the overall feel of the music.

4. Jam with Other Musicians:

- Playing with other musicians is an excellent way to develop your sense of timing and groove. It forces you to listen and adapt to the rhythm of the group.

5. Record Yourself:

   - Record yourself playing along with a metronome or backing track. Listen back to the recording to assess your timing and identify areas for improvement.

6. Practice Rhythm Exercises:

   - Practice rhythmic exercises that involve clapping or counting rhythms out loud. This helps internalize rhythmic patterns and improves your ability to feel the pulse of the music.

7. Learn Drum Patterns:

   - Learn basic drum patterns or beats. Understanding drum rhythms can enhance your understanding of groove and how different instruments contribute to the overall rhythm of a song.

8. Experiment with Dynamics:

   - Vary the dynamics (volume) of your playing to add interest and expression to your music. Experiment with playing louder and softer to create dynamic contrast.

9. Feel the Space between the Notes:

   - Pay attention to the space between the notes, known as rests. Silence and pauses are crucial elements of rhythm and groove.

10. Use Phrasing and Articulation:

   - Use different articulations, such as staccato or legato, to shape your phrases and add character to your playing.

11. Practice with Backing Tracks:

   - Play along with backing tracks that have a consistent groove. This will help you practice staying in time with a full musical accompaniment.

Strumming Techniques For Different Music Styles

Strumming techniques can vary greatly depending on the music style you want to play on the mandolin. Different genres have distinct rhythmic patterns and strumming styles that contribute to their unique sound. Here are some strumming techniques for different music styles:

1. Folk Music:

   - For folk music, use a combination of downstrokes and upstrokes in a relaxed and steady manner.

   - Employ simple strumming patterns, such as down-down-up-up-down-up, to create a laid-back and easy-going feel.

2. Bluegrass:

- In bluegrass music, focus on precision and speed in your strumming patterns.

- Use a combination of downstrokes and upstrokes in fast-paced patterns, often incorporating syncopation and rhythmic variations.

3. Country Music:

- For country music, incorporate a mix of downstrokes and upstrokes with a slight emphasis on the downbeat.

- Use more relaxed strumming patterns with occasional accentuation on specific beats.

4. Jazz Music:

- Jazz strumming often involves syncopation, swing rhythm, and more complex chord progressions.

- Experiment with various strumming patterns, including syncopated downstrokes and upstrokes, to complement the jazz feel.

5. Pop Music:

- Pop music often employs straightforward strumming patterns that follow the song's rhythm and tempo.
- Use a combination of downstrokes and upstrokes with attention to dynamics to match the song's mood.

6. Rock Music:

- In rock music, strum with more power and energy, using aggressive downstrokes and occasional upstrokes.
- Employ palm muting and other techniques to create a distinct rock sound.

7. Classical Music:

- Classical mandolin music may involve fingerpicking more than traditional strumming.

- Use fingerpicking patterns that complement the classical composition and allow for individual note articulation.

8. Blues Music:

- For blues, focus on rhythm and groove in your strumming.

- Utilize a combination of downstrokes and upstrokes with an emphasis on expressive bends and slides.

9. Reggae Music:

- Reggae strumming is characterized by a distinctive "chuck" sound and off-beat emphasis.

- Use muted downstrokes and upstrokes with a focus on the off-beats to create the reggae groove.

10. Latin Music:

- Latin music often features syncopated and rhythmic strumming patterns.

- Experiment with different patterns that match the specific Latin style you are playing, such as salsa, bossa nova, or tango.

Chapter 6: Advanced Techniques

Introduction To Advanced Techniques Like Tremolo, Slides, And Hammer-Ons.

Once you have mastered the basics of playing the mandolin, you can explore more advanced techniques to enhance your musical expression and add depth to your playing. Here are some popular advanced techniques:

1. Tremolo:
   - Tremolo is a rapid and continuous repetition of a single note, creating a sustained and shimmering effect.
   - To play tremolo on the mandolin, use your picking hand's index or middle finger to rapidly pluck the same note while keeping the other fingers lightly resting on the string for support.

- Practice tremolo slowly at first and gradually increase the speed to achieve a smooth and controlled tremolo effect.

2. Slides:

- Slides are used to smoothly transition between two notes by sliding your finger along the fretboard. Slides can be upward (ascending) or downward (descending).

- To perform a slide, start by pressing down on the first note, then without lifting your finger, slide it to the target note.

- Experiment with different slide lengths and speeds to create varying degrees of pitch glides.

3. Hammer-ons:

- Hammer-ons are a technique used to produce a note without plucking the string again. Instead, you "hammer" a finger onto the fretboard to sound the next higher note.

- To execute a hammer-on, play the initial note with a downstroke and then quickly and forcefully "hammer" the subsequent note with a finger onto the fretboard.

- Practice hammer-ons with both your index and middle fingers to develop speed and accuracy.

4. Pull-offs:

- Pull-offs are the reverse of hammer-ons. They are used to transition from a higher note to a lower note without re-plucking the string.

- To perform a pull-off, start by pressing down on the higher note, then "pluck" the string downward while simultaneously releasing your finger from the higher note to sound the lower note.

- Practice pull-offs with a smooth and fluid motion to achieve a seamless transition between the two notes.

5. Combining Techniques:

- Once you have a good grasp of these techniques individually, try combining them to create more intricate and expressive phrases in your playing.

- For example, you can combine slides with hammer-ons or pull-offs to add ornamentation and flair to your melodies.

6. Use in Melodies and Solos:

- Incorporate these advanced techniques into your melodies and solos to add dynamics, expression, and musicality to your playing.

- Experiment with different tempos, styles, and genres to see how these techniques fit within various musical contexts.

Developing Speed And Accuracy In Playing

Developing speed and accuracy in playing the mandolin is a gradual process that requires focused practice and patience. Here are some strategies to help you improve your speed and accuracy on the mandolin:

1. Start Slowly:
 - Begin practicing at a slow tempo to ensure accuracy in your playing. Focus on playing each note cleanly and precisely.

2. Use a Metronome:
 - Practice with a metronome to develop a steady sense of timing. Set the metronome to a comfortable pace and gradually increase the speed as you improve.

3. Practice Regularly:

- Consistent practice is essential for developing speed and accuracy. Set aside dedicated practice time each day to work on your technique.

4. Isolate Difficult Passages:

- Identify challenging parts in a piece or exercise and isolate them for focused practice. Slowly work on these passages until you can play them accurately.

5. Practice Finger Exercises:

- Incorporate finger exercises and drills into your practice routine. These exercises can improve finger dexterity and strength, which are crucial for playing with speed and accuracy.

6. Use Correct Finger Placement:

- Ensure that you are using the correct finger placement on the fretboard. Use the tips of your fingers to press down on the strings, and avoid touching adjacent strings unintentionally.

7. Practice Alternate Picking:

- Use alternate picking (down-up) to play single notes and scales. This technique can improve speed and control in your picking hand.

8. Practice Scales and Arpeggios:

- Regularly practice scales and arpeggios in different keys and positions on the fretboard. This will help improve your finger coordination and familiarize you with common patterns.

9. Relax Your Hands and Fingers:

- Tension in your hands and fingers can hinder speed and accuracy. Focus on staying relaxed while playing, and avoid unnecessary tension.

10. Record Yourself:

- Record yourself playing and listen back to identify areas for improvement. This can help you pinpoint specific issues in your technique and work on them effectively.

11. Be Patient and Persistent:

- Developing speed and accuracy takes time, so be patient with yourself and keep practicing consistently.

Chapter 7: Playing Simple Melody Songs On The Mandolin

As a beginner, take your time to learn each song slowly and focus on getting the chords and finger placements right. As you gain confidence and proficiency, you can explore more complex songs and techniques. Enjoy playing the mandolin!

Here are some easy and beginner-friendly songs that can be played on the mandolin:

1. "Twinkle, Twinkle, Little Star" - A classic nursery rhyme melody.

To play "Twinkle, Twinkle, Little Star" on the mandolin, you'll need to tune your mandolin to G-D-A-E, which is the standard tuning for most mandolins. The song is played in the key of C major. Here are the step-by-step instructions, including the melody and finger placement for each note:

Step 1: Become acquainted with the notes. Before we begin, let's familiarize ourselves with the notes on the mandolin fretboard. The notes on each string, from the thinnest string to the thickest, are as follows:

- 1st (E) string: E4, F4, F#4, G4, G#4, A4, A#4, B4, C5, C#5, D5, D#5, E5
- 2nd (A) string: A3, A#3, B3, C4, C#4, D4, D#4, E4, F4, F#4, G4, G#4, A4
- 3rd (D) string: D3, D#3, E3, F3, F#3, G3, G#3, A3, A#3, B3, C4, C#4, D4
- 4th (G) string: G2, G#2, A2, A#2, B2, C3, C#3, D3, D#3, E3, F3, F#3, G3

Step 2: Learn the Melody

Here's the melody for "Twinkle, Twinkle, Little Star":

(C)　(C)　(G)　(G)　(A)　(A) (G)

Twinkle, twinkle, little star

(F)　(F)　(E)　(E)　(D)　(D)　(C)

How I wonder what you are

(G)　(G)　(F)　(F)　(E)　(E)　(D)

Up above the world so high

(G)　(G)　(F)　(F)　(E)　(E) (D)

Like a diamond in the sky

(C)　(C)　(G)　(G)　(A)　(A)　(G)

Twinkle, twinkle, little star

(F)　(F)　(E)　(E)　(D)　(D)　(C)

How I wonder what you are

Step 3: Finger Placement

The numbers represent the finger placement on the fretboard. Here's how you place your fingers for each note:

- (C) - Play the C note on the 1st (E) string with your ring finger on the 3rd fret.

- (G) - Play the G note on the 2nd (A) string with your index finger on the 2nd fret.
- (A) - Play the A note on the 2nd (A) string with your middle finger on the 2nd fret.
- (F) - Play the F note on the 3rd (D) string with your index finger on the 3rd fret.
- (E) - Play the E note on the 3rd (D) string with your middle finger on the 2nd fret.
- (D) - Play the D note on the 3rd (D) string with your index finger on the 2nd fret.

Step 4: Putting It All Together

Now that you know the melody and finger placement, play each note while following the rhythm of the song. The timing of the notes should be evenly spaced, and you can use a pick or your fingers to pluck the strings.

Remember, practice makes perfect. Take your time to get familiar with the finger placement and the melody. Start slowly and gradually increase your speed as you become more comfortable.

That's it! Have fun playing "Twinkle, Twinkle, Little Star" on your mandolin!

2. "You Are My Sunshine" - A simple and heartwarming folk song.

To play "You Are My Sunshine" on the mandolin, you'll need to tune your mandolin to G-D-A-E, which is the standard tuning for most mandolins. The song is played in the key of G major. Here are the step-by-step instructions, including the melody and finger placement for each note:

Step 1: Become acquainted with the notes.
Before we begin, let's familiarize ourselves with the notes on the mandolin fretboard. The notes on each string, from the thinnest string to the thickest, are as follows:

- 1st (E) string: E4, F4, F#4, G4, G#4, A4, A#4, B4, C5, C#5, D5, D#5, E5
- 2nd (A) string: A3, A#3, B3, C4, C#4, D4, D#4, E4, F4, F#4, G4, G#4, A4

- 3rd (D) string: D3, D#3, E3, F3, F#3, G3, G#3, A3, A#3, B3, C4, C#4, D4

- 4th (G) string: G2, G#2, A2, A#2, B2, C3, C#3, D3, D#3, E3, F3, F#3, G3

Step 2: Learn the Melody

Here's the melody for "You Are My Sunshine":

(G)   (C)   (G)   (D)
You are my sunshine, my only sunshine
(G)   (C)   (G)   (D)
You make me happy when skies are gray
(G)   (C)   (G)   (D)
You'll never know, dear, how much I love you
(G)   (C)   (G)   (D)   (G)
Please don't take my sunshine away

Step 3: Finger Placement

The numbers represent the finger placement on the fretboard. Here's how you place your fingers for each note:

- (G) - Play the G note on the 4th (G) string with your index finger on the 2nd fret.
- (C) - Play the C note on the 3rd (D) string with your ring finger on the 2nd fret.
- (D) - Play the D note on the 3rd (D) string with your middle finger on the 3rd fret.

Step 4: Putting It All Together

Now that you know the melody and finger placement, play each note while following the rhythm of the song. The timing of the notes should be evenly spaced, and you can use a pick or your fingers to pluck the strings.

To play the entire song, simply repeat the melody for each verse of the lyrics.

Remember to practice slowly and gradually increase your speed as you become more comfortable with the song.

That's it! Enjoy playing "You Are My Sunshine" on your mandolin!

3. "Amazing Grace" - A beautiful and well-known hymn.

To play "Amazing Grace" on the mandolin, you'll need to tune your instrument to G-D-A-E, which is the standard tuning for most mandolins. The song is played in the key of G major. Here are the step-by-step instructions, including the melody and finger placement for each note:

Step 1: Become acquainted with the notes
Before we begin, let's familiarize ourselves with the notes on the mandolin fretboard. The notes on each string, from the thinnest string to the thickest, are as follows:

- 1st (E) string: E4, F4, F#4, G4, G#4, A4, A#4, B4, C5, C#5, D5, D#5, E5
- 2nd (A) string: A3, A#3, B3, C4, C#4, D4, D#4, E4, F4, F#4, G4, G#4, A4

- 3rd (D) string: D3, D#3, E3, F3, F#3, G3, G#3, A3, A#3, B3, C4, C#4, D4

- 4th (G) string: G2, G#2, A2, A#2, B2, C3, C#3, D3, D#3, E3, F3, F#3, G3

Step 2: Learn the Melody

Here's the melody for "Amazing Grace":

(G)   (D)   (G)   (C)   (G)
Amazing grace, how sweet the sound
(G)   (D)   (G) (Em) (D)   (G)
That saved a wretch like me
(G)   (C)   (G)   (D)   (G)
I once was lost, but now I'm found
(G)   (D)   (G)   (D)   (G)
Was blind, but now I see

Step 3: Finger Placement

The numbers represent the finger placement on the fretboard. Here's how you place your fingers for each note:

- (G) - Play the G note on the 4th (G) string with your index finger on the 2nd fret.
- (D) - Play the D note on the 3rd (D) string with your middle finger on the 2nd fret.
- (C) - Play the C note on the 3rd (D) string with your index finger on the 1st fret.
- (Em) - Play the E minor chord by placing your index finger on the 2nd fret of the 4th (G) string and your ring finger on the 2nd fret of the 2nd (A) string.

Step 4: Putting It All Together

Now that you know the melody and finger placement, play each note while following the rhythm of the song. The timing of the notes should be evenly spaced, and you can use a pick or your fingers to pluck the strings.

The chord progression for each line is: G - D - G - C - G for the first and second lines, and

G - D - G - D - G for the third and fourth lines.

Remember to practice slowly and gradually increase your speed as you become more comfortable with the song.

That's it! Enjoy playing "Amazing Grace" on your mandolin!

4. "I'll Fly Away" - A popular gospel and bluegrass song.

"I'll Fly Away" is a classic gospel song, and it sounds great on the mandolin. To play "I'll Fly Away" on the mandolin, you'll need to tune your instrument to G-D-A-E, which is the standard tuning for most mandolins. The song is played in the key of G major. Here are the step-by-step instructions, including the melody and finger placement for each note:

Step 1: Become acquainted with the notes.
Before we begin, let's familiarize ourselves with the notes on the mandolin fretboard. The notes on each string, from the thinnest string to the thickest, are as follows:

- 1st (E) string: E4, F4, F#4, G4, G#4, A4, A#4, B4, C5, C#5, D5, D#5, E5

- 2nd (A) string: A3, A#3, B3, C4, C#4, D4, D#4, E4, F4, F#4, G4, G#4, A4
- 3rd (D) string: D3, D#3, E3, F3, F#3, G3, G#3, A3, A#3, B3, C4, C#4, D4
- 4th (G) string: G2, G#2, A2, A#2, B2, C3, C#3, D3, D#3, E3, F3, F#3, G3

Step 2: Learn the Melody

Here's the main melody for "I'll Fly Away" on the mandolin:

(G)   (C) (G)   (D)   (G)
Some bright morning when this life is o'er, I'll fly away

(G)   (C) (G)   (D)   (G)
To a home on God's celestial shore, I'll fly away

Step 3: Finger Placement

The numbers represent the finger placement on the fretboard. Here's how you place your fingers for each note:

- (G) - Play the G note on the 4th (G) string with your index finger on the 2nd fret.
- (C) - Play the C note on the 3rd (D) string with your ring finger on the 2nd fret.
- (D) - Play the D note on the 3rd (D) string with your middle finger on the 3rd fret.

Step 4: Putting It All Together

Now that you know the melody and finger placement, play each note while following the rhythm of the song. The timing of the notes should be evenly spaced, and you can use a pick or your fingers to pluck the strings.

For the song structure, simply repeat the melody for each verse and chorus.

5. "Scarborough Fair" - A traditional English ballad with an easy chord progression.

"Scarborough Fair" is a traditional English folk song that has been covered by many artists over the years. To play "Scarborough Fair" on the mandolin, you'll need to tune your instrument to G-D-A-E, which is the standard tuning for most mandolins. The song is played in the key of D minor. Here are the step-by-step instructions, including the melody and finger placement for each note:

Step 1: Become acquainted with the notes
Before we begin, let's familiarize ourselves with the notes on the mandolin fretboard. The notes on each string, from the thinnest string to the thickest, are as follows:

- 1st (E) string: E4, F4, F#4, G4, G#4, A4, A#4, B4, C5, C#5, D5, D#5, E5
- 2nd (A) string: A3, A#3, B3, C4, C#4, D4, D#4, E4, F4, F#4, G4, G#4, A4
- 3rd (D) string: D3, D#3, E3, F3, F#3, G3, G#3, A3, A#3, B3, C4, C#4, D4
- 4th (G) string: G2, G#2, A2, A#2, B2, C3, C#3, D3, D#3, E3, F3, F#3, G3

Step 2: Learn the Melody

Here's the main melody for "Scarborough Fair" on the mandolin:

(Dm)   (C)   (Bb)   (F)
(A)
Are you going to Scarborough Fair? Parsley, sage, rosemary, and thyme
(Dm)   (C)   (Bb)   (F)
(A)
Remember me to one who lives there, she once was a true love of mine

Step 3: Finger Placement

The numbers represent the finger placement on the fretboard. Here's how you place your fingers for each note:

- (Dm) - Play the D minor chord by placing your index finger on the 2nd fret of the 4th (G) string and your ring finger on the 2nd fret of the 1st (E) string.
- (C) - Play the C chord by placing your index finger on the 1st fret of the 4th (G) string and your middle finger on the 2nd fret of the 2nd (A) string.
- (Bb) - Play the Bb chord by placing your index finger on the 1st fret of the 3rd (D) string and your ring finger on the 3rd fret of the 1st (E) string.
- (F) - Play the F chord by placing your index finger on the 1st fret of the 2nd (A) string, your middle finger on the 2nd fret of

the 3rd (D) string, and your ring finger on the 3rd fret of the 4th (G) string.

- (A) - Play the A chord by placing your index finger on the 2nd fret of the 3rd (D) string and your ring finger on the 2nd fret of the 1st (E) string.

Step 4: Putting It All Together

Now that you know the melody and finger placement, play each note while following the rhythm of the song. The timing of the notes should be evenly spaced, and you can use a pick or your fingers to pluck the strings.

The chord progression for each line is: Dm - C - Bb - F - A.

Remember to practice slowly and gradually increase your speed as you become more comfortable with the song.

6. "Wildwood Flower" - A classic bluegrass tune with simple picking patterns.

"Wildwood Flower" is a traditional American folk song, and it sounds lovely on the mandolin. To play "Wildwood Flower" on the mandolin, you'll need to tune your instrument to G-D-A-E, which is the standard tuning for most mandolins. The song is played in the key of G major. Here are the step-by-step instructions, including the melody and finger placement for each note:

Step 1: Become acquainted with the notes
Before we begin, let's familiarize ourselves with the notes on the mandolin fretboard. The notes on each string, from the thinnest string to the thickest, are as follows:

- 1st (E) string: E4, F4, F#4, G4, G#4, A4, A#4, B4, C5, C#5, D5, D#5, E5
- 2nd (A) string: A3, A#3, B3, C4, C#4, D4, D#4, E4, F4, F#4, G4, G#4, A4
- 3rd (D) string: D3, D#3, E3, F3, F#3, G3, G#3, A3, A#3, B3, C4, C#4, D4
- 4th (G) string: G2, G#2, A2, A#2, B2, C3, C#3, D3, D#3, E3, F3, F#3, G3

Step 2: Learn the Melody

Here's the main melody for "Wildwood Flower" on the mandolin:

(G)   (G)   (G)   (G)
Oh, I'll twine with my mingles and waving black hair
(G)   (C)   (G)   (D)
With the roses so red and the lilies so fair
(G)   (G)   (G)   (G)
And the myrtle so bright with an emerald hue

(G)   (D)   (G)   (G)

The pale and the leader and eyes look like blue

Step 3: Finger Placement

The numbers represent the finger placement on the fretboard. Here's how you place your fingers for each note:

- (G) - Play the G note on the 4th (G) string with your index finger on the 2nd fret.
- (C) - Play the C note on the 3rd (D) string with your ring finger on the 2nd fret.
- (D) - Play the D note on the 3rd (D) string with your middle finger on the 3rd fret.

Step 4: Putting It All Together

Now that you know the melody and finger placement, play each note while following the rhythm of the song. The timing of the notes should be evenly spaced, and you can use a pick or your fingers to pluck the strings.

The chord progression for each line is: G - G - G - G - G - C - G - D - G.

7. "House of the Rising Sun" - A haunting folk song made famous by The Animals.

"House of the Rising Sun" is a classic folk song that has been covered by various artists over the years. It's often played in the key of Am (A minor) on the mandolin. To play "House of the Rising Sun" on the mandolin, you'll need to tune your instrument to G-D-A-E, which is the standard tuning for most mandolins. Here are the step-by-step instructions, including the melody and finger placement for each note:

Step 1: Become acquainted with the notes
Before we begin, let's familiarize ourselves with the notes on the mandolin fretboard. The notes on each string, from the thinnest string to the thickest, are as follows:

- 1st (E) string: E4, F4, F#4, G4, G#4, A4, A#4, B4, C5, C#5, D5, D#5, E5
- 2nd (A) string: A3, A#3, B3, C4, C#4, D4, D#4, E4, F4, F#4, G4, G#4, A4
- 3rd (D) string: D3, D#3, E3, F3, F#3, G3, G#3, A3, A#3, B3, C4, C#4, D4
- 4th (G) string: G2, G#2, A2, A#2, B2, C3, C#3, D3, D#3, E3, F3, F#3, G3

Step 2: Learn the Melody

Here's the main melody for "House of the Rising Sun" on the mandolin:

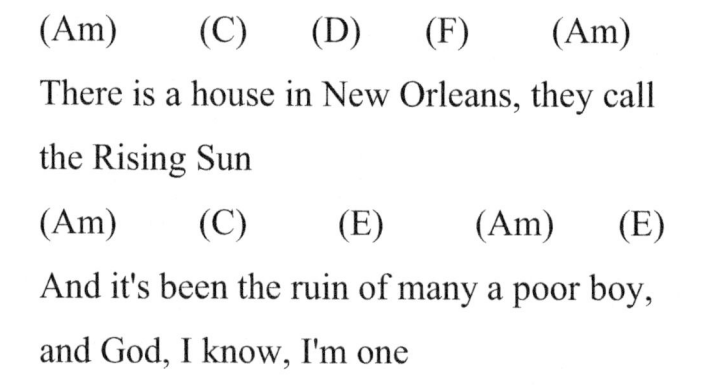

(Am)   (C)   (D)   (F)   (Am)
There is a house in New Orleans, they call the Rising Sun
(Am)   (C)   (E)   (Am)   (E)
And it's been the ruin of many a poor boy, and God, I know, I'm one

Step 3: Finger Placement

The numbers represent the finger placement on the fretboard. Here's how you place your fingers for each note:

- (Am) - Play the A minor chord by placing your index finger on the 2nd fret of the 4th (G) string and your ring finger on the 2nd fret of the 1st (E) string.
- (C) - Play the C chord by placing your index finger on the 1st fret of the 4th (G) string and your middle finger on the 2nd fret of the 2nd (A) string.
- (D) - Play the D chord by placing your index finger on the 2nd fret of the 3rd (D) string and your ring finger on the 3rd fret of the 2nd (A) string.
- (F) - Play the F chord by placing your index finger on the 1st fret of the 2nd (A) string and your middle finger on the 2nd fret of the 3rd (D) string.

- (E) - Play the E chord by placing your index finger on the 1st fret of the 3rd (D) string and your middle finger on the 2nd fret of the 1st (E) string.

Step 4: Putting It All Together

Now that you know the melody and finger placement, play each note while following the rhythm of the song. The timing of the notes should be evenly spaced, and you can use a pick or your fingers to pluck the strings.

The chord progression for each line is: Am - C - D - F - Am - Am - C - E - Am - E.

Remember to practice slowly and gradually increase your speed as you become more comfortable with the song.

Chapter 8: Maintenance And Care

Properly Maintaining Your Mandolin To Ensure Longevity

Properly maintaining your mandolin is essential to ensure its longevity and keep it in excellent playing condition. Here are some tips for maintaining your mandolin:

1. Keep it Clean:

- Regularly clean your mandolin after each playing session. Use a soft, lint-free cloth to wipe off any dirt, dust, or sweat from the instrument's surface, strings, and fretboard.

2. Store it Properly:

- When not in use, store your mandolin in a suitable case or a mandolin stand. Proper storage protects it from dust, humidity, and accidental damage.

3. Avoid Extreme Temperatures and Humidity:

   - Mandolins are sensitive to extreme temperatures as well as humidity. Avoid leaving your mandolin in direct sunlight, near heaters, or in damp environments.

   - Consider using a humidifier during dry seasons to maintain optimal humidity levels for the instrument.

4. Tune Up Regularly:

   - Tune your mandolin regularly to maintain proper string tension and prevent undue stress on the instrument. Invest in a good quality tuner for accurate tuning.

5. Change Strings When Necessary:

   - Replace your mandolin strings periodically, as they can lose their brightness and elasticity over time. How often you need to change the strings depends on how frequently you play and your preference for tone.

6. Check and Adjust Action:

   - The action (height of the strings above the fretboard) affects playability. If you notice any buzzing or difficulty fretting notes, have a professional luthier check and adjust the action.

7. Monitor the Neck and Fretboard:

   - Regularly inspect the neck and fretboard for any signs of warping, cracks, or wear. If you notice any issues, consult a skilled luthier for repairs.

8. Clean the Fretboard:

   - Clean the fretboard occasionally using a soft, damp cloth. Avoid using harsh chemicals or excessive water, as this may damage the wood.

9. Use a Guitar/Mandolin Stand During Breaks:

- When taking breaks during practice sessions or performances, use a mandolin stand to support the instrument. Avoid leaning it against walls or furniture, as this may cause accidents and damage.

Cleaning, Restringing, And Adjusting The Instrument

Cleaning, restringing, and adjusting your mandolin are important maintenance tasks that can help keep your instrument in top condition and ensure it continues to produce the best sound possible. Here's a step-by-step guide for each process:

Cleaning Your Mandolin:

1. Gather Supplies:
   - Soft, lint-free cloths
   - Guitar/musical instrument polish (if applicable)
   - Mild, non-abrasive guitar/musical instrument cleaner (if applicable)

2. Remove Dust and Dirt:

   - Use a soft, dry cloth to gently wipe off any dust or dirt from the body, neck, and headstock of the mandolin.

3. Clean the Fretboard:

   - If needed, use a slightly damp cloth to clean the fretboard. Avoid using excessive water, as moisture can damage the wood.

4. Polish the Finish (Optional):

   - If your mandolin has a glossy finish, you can apply a small amount of guitar/musical instrument polish on a soft cloth and gently buff the surface to restore its shine.

5. Check Hardware and Fasteners:

   - Inspect the tuning machines, tailpiece, and bridge for any loose screws or fasteners. Tighten them if necessary, but be gentle to avoid damaging the instrument.

Restringing Your Mandolin:

1. Select the Right Strings:
   - Choose high-quality mandolin strings that suit your playing style and preferences. Common tunings for a mandolin are GDAE (standard) or CGDA (octave).

2. Remove Old Strings:
   - One at a time, loosen the tension on the old strings and unwind them from the tuning pegs.
   - Dispose of old strings responsibly.

3. Clean the Instrument:
   - While the strings are off, take the opportunity to clean the fretboard and other parts of the mandolin if needed.

4. Install New Strings:

- Begin by threading the new string through the tailpiece, then through the bridge.

- Wind the string around the appropriate tuning peg and ensure it sits securely in the nut.

5. Stretch and Tune the Strings:

- After installing all the new strings, gently stretch each one by pulling it away from the fretboard and retuning it several times until it holds its pitch.

Adjusting Your Mandolin:

1. Check Action and Neck Relief:

 - Evaluate the action (string height) and neck relief (bow in the neck) of your mandolin. Both factors impact playability and intonation.

 - For significant adjustments, it's best to consult a professional luthier.

2. Adjust the Truss Rod (Advanced):

 - If your mandolin has a truss rod and you're experienced with instrument adjustments, you can adjust the neck relief to achieve the desired action.

3. Adjust the Bridge (Advanced):

 - To fine-tune the action, you can adjust the bridge height slightly, ensuring that each string is at the desired height.

4. Check Intonation:

- Play the mandolin at various positions on the fretboard and check if the intonation (correct pitch) is accurate.

- If necessary, adjust the bridge position to achieve better intonation.

Note:

- If you're not confident about adjusting your mandolin, it's best to seek help from a professional luthier or technician.

By regularly cleaning, restringing, and maintaining your mandolin, you'll ensure its longevity and enjoy the best possible sound quality while playing.

Dealing With Common Issues And Troubleshooting

Dealing with common issues and troubleshooting is an essential skill for any mandolin player. Here are some common issues you might encounter and how to address them:

1. String Buzz or Rattle:

- String buzz can be caused by low action, uneven frets, or worn-out strings.
- Check the action and neck relief. If they are off, consider adjusting the truss rod or bridge height.
- If the frets are uneven, consult a professional luthier for a fret leveling and dressing.

2. Tuning Stability Issues:

- Tuning stability problems can result from old or low-quality strings, improperly wound strings, or slipping tuning pegs.
- Replace old or worn-out strings with new ones of good quality.
- Make sure to wind the strings properly around the tuning pegs, with each turn overlapping the previous one to ensure a secure grip.
- If tuning pegs slip, consider applying a small amount of peg compound or replacing the tuners if necessary.

3. High Action or Difficult Fretting:

- High action can make it challenging to fret notes and play comfortably.
- Check the action at the nut and bridge. If it's too high, consider adjusting the bridge height or having the nut slots properly filed by a luthier.

4. Intonation Problems:

- Intonation issues result in notes being out of tune at various positions on the fretboard.

- Check the intonation by playing harmonics at the 12th fret and comparing them to the fretted notes. Adjust the bridge position if needed.

5. Electronics Issues (If Applicable):

- If your mandolin has a pickup or preamp, occasional electronic issues may arise.

- Check the battery for active electronics and replace it if necessary.

- If there are problems with the output or sound, inspect the cable and connections.

6. Cracks or Damage to the Wood:

- Inspect your mandolin regularly for any cracks or damage to the wood.

- If you find any cracks, take your instrument to a professional luthier for assessment and repair.

7. Fret Wear:

- Over time, frets can wear down, causing notes to buzz or intonation problems.

- If fret wear is extensive, consult a luthier for fret replacement or dressing.

8. Lack of Volume or Sustain:

- If your mandolin lacks volume or sustain, consider changing to a higher quality set of strings that suit your playing style.

- Check the setup and bridge height to ensure proper transmission of vibrations.

9. Scratchy or Stiff Tuning Pegs:

- Lubricate the tuning pegs with graphite or peg compound to improve smoothness.

Printed in Great Britain
by Amazon